**B
N
P**

BEST NEW POETS

2025

50 Poems from Emerging Writers

Cecily Parks, Guest Editor
Jeb Livingood, Series Editor

This book is published in cooperation with the University of Virginia Press (upress.virginia.edu).

For additional information, visit us at
bestnewpoets.org
facebook.com/BestNewPoets

Text set in Adobe Garamond Pro and Droid Sans

Printed by Lightning Source

ISBN: 979-8-9917112-1-0
ISSN: 1554-7019

Contents

About *Best New Poets*.. ix

Anya Kirshbaum, Letter from the Edge of Every Known Thing.................................1

Harrison Hamm, Ghost of a Peacock 2

Dora Prieto, Girls of the Now [Garments] 3

José Felipe Ozuna, Undocumented Sonnet 6

Jupiter Nesky, Kiddush Levana...7

Jessica Bowdoin, Wintering 10

Caroline Laganas, Champagne or Maggots? 12

James Ciano, The Committee of Men (Haze)..14

Lenna Mendoza, You can't really *clean* the piercing gun at Claire's, ...18

Janiru Liyanage, The Deer 19

L. A. Johnson, Birthmark 20

Brooke Middlebrook, Après L'Ondée 22

Nur Turkmani, Animal Grief 24

Peter LaBerge, California Avenue 26

emet ezell, Has Your Spirit Dried Up?..28

Kent Leatham, America's Last Hometown 29

Sam Bailey, Why I'm a Xtian..32

Cate Lycurgus, Martingale..33

Lindsay Li, 悲怆五阶段 (heritage study)..34

Genevieve Watson, Last Supper 36

Elizabeth Loudon, Renunciation 38

Courtney DuChene, On Culling...40

Brittany Male, Case Study 42

Justin Rigamonti, Failure...44

Brian Czyzyk, Equinox 46

Mckendy Fils-Aimé, the lougawou discusses repetition 48

Jackie Sabbagh, Having a Great Time Being Transgender in America Lately 50

Sophie Pedersen, feast on your life 51

Mary Spooner, Here in My Unincorporated Plot 54

Michael Hurley , Vespers or Orison or Haven 56

D. M. Spratley, The Collector of Debts..58

Alejandro Lucero, When I search "Sapello," 60

Acie Clark, Self-Portrait as Orpheus on T 62

Mason Wray, After Birds..63

Laura Cresté, Between 5,000 and 12,000 Years After the Eruption...........................66

Jonathan Diaz, Your Old Men Shall Dream Dreams, Your Young Men Shall See Visions.....................67

Rachel Rothenberg, Blessings over the Bodies of My Father's Murderers 68

Shelly Stewart Cato, River, Heron, Doe 70

Letitia Chan, Inheritance...72

Katey Funderburgh, Dinner Party 74

G.H. Plaag, Televised 76

Alexander Lee, Memorial Day & How We Fight 78

Kate DeLay, Repair..80

Chi Pham, Italian Lambskin Leather Gloves 81

Tobi Kassim, Heavyweight...84

Jen Siraganian, Thinking About My Father's Erector Set from 1948 86

Melissa McKinstry, Late Spring Epiphany After the Georgia O'Keeffe Exhibit 88

Benjamin Voigt, Grief...90

Lo Naylor, object permanence...92

Hannah Kosak, Portrait Returning to the Fog.....................................94

Acknowledgments..97

Contributors' Notes...99

Participating Magazines...109

Participating Programs..115

About *Best New Poets*

Welcome to *Best New Poets 2025*, our twenty-first annual anthology of fifty poems from emerging writers. At *Best New Poets* we define "emerging writer" narrowly: our anthology only features poets who have not yet published a book-length collection of their own poetry. Our goal is to provide special encouragement and recognition to poets just starting in their careers, the many writing programs they attend, and the magazines that publish their work.

From February to May of 2025, *Best New Poets* accepted nominations from writing programs and magazines in the United States and Canada. Each program and magazine could nominate two writers, and those poets could send a free submission to the anthology. For a small entry fee, writers could also submit poems as part of our open competition. Eligible poems were either published after January 1, 2024, or unpublished. Which means you are not only reading new poets in this book, but also some of their most recent work.

In all, we received a total of nearly three thousand poems. A pool of readers and the series editor evaluated these submissions, sending just under two hundred selections to this year's guest editor, Cecily Parks, who chose the final fifty poems that appear here.

Anya Kirshbaum
Letter from the Edge of Every Known Thing

Dear Ginkgo, are we so different? You at the edge of undress
—I, undone, unkempt, infant at my breast. I have this wild hair
curling around my neck & you—wind through your near-spent, your
yellow flare, like a body on the brink. Dear Ginkgo, whose faces
I have searched as if looking for a lighthouse on each leaf; or somewhere
a salvation pressed into your trunk. You, whose leaves have rattled
the grief-noise away—I have a mouth, I have these two hands
—what use are they? Each season I take your note, try my best
at translation. How gently you hold the birds, so carefully. Dear
Ginkgo, you riot of saffron storms, you shelter in the grief-mist.
I dreamt my father sat in your branches—watching me. You
whose life will far outlast ours—what do you think of me,
finally, so late, mothering? My nipples ache, my daughter all new,
her impossible face. Oh Ginkgo, you who have been my companion
through this avalanche of birth & departure: the two of them
crisscrossing the sky behind you. I have fingers to tear into the bread,
a hunger. I have a solemn face in the night, in the hidden rooms;
my body a laboratory of milk & lullabies. Dear Gingko, scraping
the whimpery windows through which I peer, thank you—
even when your branches shake—leaf for leaf for hair for breath
for root for feet, you eat with your whole body—a thousand rhythms
breaking, baring, rustling, shaking. Oh Ginkgo, thank you—my father
watches me, watching you, sits in your branches as starlight
on my daughter's face, as mist, as droplets of rain. Dear
Ginkgo, each leaf cleft—when some of them fall
they divide like wings.

Harrison Hamm
Ghost of a Peacock

How he gawked the lawn. How he whipped the planeteria of his blue-green train—so casually pulled like a petticoat over his head. How he died one mid-August after school. Throat purple with song. The bus driver's downcast squint when she told us, and after this, stopped coming back to the wooded church. Swear I saw him there: catwalking past green upholstered pews, shocking, turning every stray eye at the altar call. Collecting galaxies. Added them, like jewels, to a secret slit in the dress. Before dark. Before tadpoles or tragedy. Before we could follow him into the free reign of no ceiling, nothing to ribcage. Hollow then flight. Cattails bent in the slight wind. And how he ate raspberries from our still-believing hands. How suede patchouli. How god-awful iridescent it was to see his cold breath clipped. Daylight blued. His feathers all over the backyard morning. Poplar wall before the silent car. Before surrender. Before going inside. Followed his paramour into the whitening of treetops, fanned his deck of cards, angel numbers. How sometimes, I still see him. At the library. Between pages ripped apart, unread. Stoplight before runway. On the red-eye flight's plane window. Pool ball shot into table pocket. This cedared un-stillness. Shuffling the musk, the muslin like it meant nothing. Dirt driveway. The harp buried, never played. How he made an omen of himself. Of this rusted water tower town. Looking for that girl. Never larkspur. Never me.

Dora Prieto
Girls of the Now [Garments]

> *Clothes are a better place for girls to keep their histories than stories.*
> —Anne Boyer

My favorite shoe brand is telling me to "take up space." Subject line, email ad.

I am in my bikini and my armpits are sweaty.

My father is talking, in the way he does.

We are sitting by a desert hot spring near his home in central mexico.

I archive the ad, vaguely aware of his points:

Elections, yucatán, his mother's strength, his father, missing.

A monologue, a "talking to oneself " (late Latin) a declaration of his refusal to collaborate.

I psychoanalyze my father and all his secrets—but what do I know?

I am a silly little girl, which is both true and untrue.

It's true in the sense that I am, despite my best efforts, north american.

Which means I am a girl believing lug sole boots and therapy could solve my emotional heritage.

The chunky military sole, reinforced leather toe, visible seams—

Today is the day I will heal!!!

Come on, I know girls are powerful.

When Kendall Jenner said does anybody even use snapchat anymore, the platform lost millions of users
within twenty-four hours.

And in mexico city, Dua Lipa has made the lines long.

While the wall at the border is being built again.

Girls like these can change the shapes of cities with their joy.

When the ideals of consumerism align with the ideals of feminism.

I remember being relieved when we all started hating girl bosses.

Then: where does the high femme nihilism that replaced it take us?

I am sucking a mango pit; I toss the skin to the side.

There is no better time to leisurely contemplate gender than the peaceful white noise of a monologue.

I believe in the power of garments.

The crimson clasp, the bone-pleat detail, the soft cotton gusset.

See, there does exist a badass shoe, I wear it and my gender changes.

I won't tell you the brand; a poem isn't an ad.

Poems are ads for quitting your job.

Take up space, I say to myself in the bathroom mirror.

The stain of mango juice on my lips, a seam that bears memory:

As kids, we'd rub the pits all over our bodies like bars of sticky soap and then jump in the pool, washing it all away, to the distress of the nearby families.

Nasty little cochina rural canada things we were.

Before I was born, my mom had a shotgun hanging by the door.

That was her version of the boots.

She'd grab it to slug down birds for dinner or scare someone off.

She called it her husband, as in, don't make me go get my husband.

The ad offers a cheap version of this recklessness.

My mother's legacy as a wood worker, a lobster fisherman, hand work in the evenings.

I do hard labor jobs, I become a wildlands firefighter.

I get two degrees, become highly trained at synthesizing and speaking when called on.

And I buy silks, silvers, jean, sparkle spandex, linen weaves, a west coast dad fleece.

Is it all a kind of performance, even when it's real?

A girl can be a first-gen grad, bilingual; a girl can work at it all.

A savvy promise drifts by on the breeze:

Illegible bodies can still be bodies of work.

The gun goes off. The hunter returns.

Three pheasants, stars retreating, in her hand.

José Felipe Ozuna

Undocumented Sonnet

In the dream every bird is wet with blood
and leaves red clouds hanging in the sky, blue-
less and dark now that the sun has been ashed.
Today an uncle told me he shot down
a bird by making his fingers into a gun
and yelling *POW!* I don't believe dreams
are anything more than a blank page in which
your brain makes meaning out of the day.
But when the birds fell, I opened my mouth,
swallowed as many as I could. I can't explain it.
Why I still believe this country will one day grant me
anything other than contempt.
Or why I woke with feathers in my teeth.
Or why I reached for the water by my bed and drank.

—Nominated by *Muzzle Magazine*

Jupiter Nesky

Kiddush Levana

for Sydney Kito Tyler / after Natalie Diaz

Once, in a dream (was it day
or night?) I stood

in a field of flowers
and waited for

the end. I woke
in English class,

blinking. You know how it is—
I was a girl who aspired

to formlessness. Echoing,
esoteric, ephemeral.

An autistic writer I know
wrote a story once

about Godhood, a great story
I don't remember.

We (autistic) are so creative,
I remember thinking,

until a flash of sunlight
reminded me

what I was—a poet
who hates sound, sense, touch.

On the couch, singing.
In the garden, singing.

There are forces beyond,
the writer said in their low voice.

Not the day, not the night,
not elation or justice,

not eldritch, not anger,
not a star or a syllable.

Not silence or synonym
or war or scatter, or the names

they call us, not *retard*
or *retarded,*

not slow, not
slow, not a sign

or a sigh, not simple,
something serious.

The end? I asked.
Yes, they said. I mean the end.

In the garden, tying knots
into blades of grass.

In bed, the fan spinning
above me.

At school, sobbing
in my desk.

My God.
My God.

Where to go from here?
What sun lily or moon flower?

What tremble? What trembled?
What trembling?

What end? I asked them.
The end end.

—Nominated by *Glass Poetry*

Jessica Bowdoin
Wintering

"She is   "Wintering," he said,
   abuzz
   with skull thunder."   "she is hardening

                                        her skin, exoskeleton
                                        of scarred growth:
                                        overgrown,
                                        preparation for shedding."

"She has not left
   her apartment
   for months now. Her bed slumps
   into   Exuviae dreams:
   a body-shaped rut
   of dry skin and slivering   "I am wintering,"

                                        she said: "Do you mind
                                        if I knit scar wings
                                        while we talk? My next pair
                                        is a reincarnation
                                        called Root Rot
                                        and Burrow;

rot."   No,

                                        Root Rot and Ascend.
                                        I will stitch them to my skin
                                        after my exoskeleton earthquakes,

and I shimmy,
nails in bark."

"When I have dragged myself
out of myself,
only then
can we talk of abandoned

"Husks
like harvest moons

selves
sprung muddy

born of tunnels
and roots. Hear my whipstitched

and the beat of wings."

wings,
a cascade of tymbal,
and cracked-rib-singing."

Caroline Laganas
Champagne or Maggots?

People think you need a wedding or a Friday night
       to throw a party but what if all you need
is one phone call, like the one from the pathologist
       who until now you thought was someone who studied paths
but since diagnoses can only go one way
       or another, Dr. Chamberlin is the one
to tell you which treacherous track your body will take,
       and it rarely involves crossing rivers of milk
leading to ricotta lakes, or fountains spouting
       Chianti, and when it rains, it never rains
ravioli, so you go full Italian the same way
       your great-grandfather turned his backyard into the land
he abandoned—an ideal place for a garden
       where San Marzano tomatoes swell with sunshine
and blossom into a marinara sauce that tastes
       like a slow-cooked Sunday afternoon, bursting
with Aunt Caterina's cackle when Uncle Charlie
       tells a raunchy joke he heard at the barber shop—
but they haven't been around for decades, so for now,
       you try to feel for the six-millimeter mass
the radiologist discovered in your left breast
       but decide to make spaghetti with pecorino
and pepper instead, because joy is not a crumb
       but a rum cake your grandmother made extra boozy
by doubling the amount of Bacardi Dark—
       meanwhile, you wish you could change the song Pandora plays

while you're trapped inside the MRI machine—
        as if Taylor Swift singing "Bad Blood" is what you need
to hear right now as the surgeon prepares the needle
        that's going to plumb your numb breast, and why do people
always think you need good music at a party
        when all you need is your mother's breath warming your name
or your grandmother saying *I made you lasagne,*
        because after all, death is either a long meal
alone with maggots and stinkbugs or a table set
        with champagne and strawberries, cacio e pepe,
bistecca alla fiorentina, and gelato
        for you and everyone you've ever loved to share
for eternity, so when the phone finally rings
        you take the champagne off ice and pop the bottle
because your biopsy results are benign
        and you're ready to crank up Frank Sinatra's
"I've Got the World on a String" and dance in the spotlight
        of the refrigerator's open door all night.

James Ciano
The Committee of Men (Haze)

A thick sheet all the way to the ocean
turns the sun

the kind of light
that my mother's first cigarette of the day

would turn the kitchen,
6am, sitting in the ashtray.

My mother at the table
eating a bowl of cereal,

dishes in the sink,
glazed where the fat hardened.

Smoke that rose to the ceiling fan
then blew into my bedroom,

which, as I woke, had the blur
of a quickly taken photo.

There were no photos when Kevin
asked for his mother, and no one

answered, that night we were initiated
as members of the soccer team.

When his eyes stopped reeling
like slots in his head

there was a sudden inner dynamism
to his body and then

a sudden outer stillness
to the basement, where his body

lay motionless on the floor.
Earlier, to prove our worth,

we were locked in a bathroom
coated with shit,

then blindfolded, force fed
American cheese, vodka, and cinnamon.

The mountains are gone this morning.
The last downtown at the edge

of the world only a faint outline
graffitied to the sky.

I haven't forgotten you, Kevin.
I held your face in my hands.

I held your body over the trashcan.
Who did I want to become,

shirtless, unable to stand,
the tiles brined with silt

where we were waterboarded
with Milwaukee's Best.

Stair-runs with Dubra and glasses
of milk, heads held in buckets

of ice, then punched,
then my mouth held open.

What did I want to belong to?
I am here in Los Angeles

where the air is difficult to breathe today.
I'm on a new medication

that makes my life feel weightless,
a kind of floating, like I can reach anything

with my hand—I know that,
but in my hand each thing already

has the quality of memory,
that light, and inaccurate.

I never said yes,
but I also never said no.

Did it enlarge my life to survive?
Did I feel pride? What did I feel,

unsure if Kevin on the floor
was alive? After several minutes

he came back into his body.
He asked for his mom.

No one called his mom.
We all laughed and smacked each other

on the ass.
Kevin sat up, dripping with sweat.

Music was put on and other people came,
and Kevin sat.

We gave him a bottle of water.
We gave him a beer.

Lenna Mendoza

You can't really clean *the piercing gun at Claire's,*

so I got some of every girl who came before me: the hushed Catholic
school transfer, home bakers and body sprayers, bullies who became

nurses. Vacation Bible School and platform shoe girls, girls who shot
the shit and bucks beside their brothers, cops' daughters, track walkers,

the girls who'd marry my crushes, the girls who blew my crushes
to bits when they mocked "I Kissed a Girl," the gay girls I didn't know

I knew. We all winced in the bar-height chair, our backs to glass,
second guessed the cheap studs we'd selected for six weeks' wear.

Our nubs of tissue held and hole-punched by a slightly older teen
with two weeks' training. That pinch of blood we shared

too much for my friend who dutifully dabbed saline-drenched cotton
and still wound up with pus and crust. My left hole closed

from underuse, begged more blunt-force abuse. The gunslinger
talked up her aim when it was done, came in close for a better view.

The wince I wore succumbed to her cherry blossom perfume,
antisepticized by the alcohol on which the scent flew.

Months elapsed, I swapped the stud for a fishhook back, and then I knew:
she'd forked the piercing's exit wound, marked me in my twoness.

Janiru Liyanage
The Deer

It stands in the clearing we enter,
my father and I, on the hottest day of June,
in a nature sanctuary, forty minutes from our apartment.
So silent and still, my father says
it's fake, some hollow plastic prop that'll fool no one
but me—my father, like all men,
an expert in everything
until the deer's ear twitches and my father, like any boy, starts shouting:
It's real! You don't see, no? It's real!
The last time he saw one,
his mother had just died. He believed it was her. It fled,
and he stopped believing in anything altogether.
He takes a photo with the flash, but the deer doesn't flinch,
stunned like a word waiting for its meaning.
Meanwhile, my mother is in our apartment, rippling under her migraine—
her damp dark body cooled against the sheets, coiling like a comma.
Like all men, I write about my mother as if she is punctuation:
here only to clarify this world being built. Once, my father's mother
dragged my mother to the shrine of her cloven-footed idol
to pray for my mother's fertility, and when my mother tells
her version of the story, all she remembers is the priest
taking another woman inside, and the woman
leaving with her face streaked in semen. How else to say this?
In the end, my father and I, like all men,
streaked in sweat, are just animals,
who eat other animals. This is why the deer doesn't move.
It is afraid of us. And we are afraid of the deer
leaving, and what we'd do
with ourselves when it's gone.

L. A. Johnson
Birthmark

In California, even the worst
is forgiven: flooding roads
lead to freeway superbloom, birds
make nests out of all our trash.
And despite drought, jacarandas
spike purple in July, their roots
cracking the concrete. Once,
I tripped under one, tore the skin
off my knees. And at last removed
the leftover scars of childhood.
My father fell once outside
the dirtiest apartment I lived in
that overlooked the freeway
on a street where no one walked.
Yet when he fell, some kind stranger
materialized out of the smog
and lifted him to his feet.
I thought then it was an accident,
the stranger a good omen,
and raised no alarm over what
I would call now his *thin legs*.
But there's no tree to bloom
from his grave, his body
the opposite of a seed. When
I can no longer bear the weight,
I declutter my closet, my drawers.
Beneath a jacaranda, I leave

my abandoned items on the sidewalk,
and in only hours, my mistakes
are absorbed by the city.
Tonight, with the objects gone,
I try to think of my regrets
with tenderness, handling them
the way someone who loves me
might touch an old scar.

Brooke Middlebrook
Après L'Ondée

I began collecting perfume samples | after

I moved to Houston, not realizing that the sweltering heat, | the

humidity, the frequent | rain

dampened movement of scent molecules to one's nose. There were | signs

that acquiring new perfume was becoming an obsession, tiny glass vials | everywhere

in my apartment, until I heard someone | saying

the best way to organize them was in ammo boxes. | you

could keep them safe from heat and light, an easy place to store all your | loot

After the hurricane, some of us wanted to live life differently, didn't | we

I suddenly found myself craving green scents, like the fresh growth of a new | shoot.

the hurricane, a chemical plant full of unstable peroxides not far from
  city lost power, flooded from a record amount of pelting
    Residents were told to evacuate because without AC, all
      pointed to imminent combustion and explosion. But
      the water rose, the roads impassable. Workers had been
      for years it wasn't safe, but
      know big companies, they're only thinking about profits, precious
    Watching the news as the chemicals finally broke down,
  exhaled sharply when we saw the flames
into the sky, the velvet-black smoke, nothing to do now but breathe in.

—Nominated by *The Cincinnati Review*

Nur Turkmani
Animal Grief

A golden jackal returns to the border town of Aitaroun
after a year of phosphorus. June, wasn't it,
years ago when we swam in the opal sea of Naqoura,
also a border town. How strange to be thirty
and for those words *years* and *ago* to bear such weight.
Do you remember? We had fish.
Split open pomegranates and lazed into the afternoon.
On our way home to Beirut, the sky curious like a face,
you said border towns are the most beautiful:
their existence depends on make-believe.
Like us they inherit illusion,
then displacement.
The jackal's ancestor was the two-million-year-old river dog
roaming what is now southern Europe.
A fossil found near Beirut tells us this.
Now its descendant stands in a field after a war that is over,
but not yet. Jackal from the Turkish çakal,
from the Persian šagāl, this legacy of naming—
or theft. The disappointment of the jackal's gaze.
What does it see that we don't?
All day I've wondered about you,
your orchards, the orange and lemon trees in the heat,
your ache trapped like a root.
Of all the things I can envy a jackal for—
its instinct to mate for life,
the shed of its coat from red to tawny dark,
the trot of its feet, slipping into valleys and forests

to feign a perfect death—
it is the howl that haunts me.
The rise and fall of sound as midday descends to night,
and night becomes chorus. I imagine us on the Naqoura cliff,
the jackal above. A wail thin as wind. We imitate it.
Hesitant as we've been taught to be until
without warning our lungs yield.
A cry, wild and guttural,
rips through towns and settlements,
hurling the language off our chest, this room we've tucked terror in,
this terror that knows no borders,
every stone and trunk hurtling down river valleys,
over gorges, past the falls, we howl and howl and howl
into the livid mouth of a year.

Peter LaBerge
California Avenue

Palo Alto, California

Boys are calling the hotline just before midnight, naked
in the white-wicker mouths of bedroom closets. They are
paying out of pocket for the emergency tests.

They wanted the evening until they were full of what
it became. And you are seeding them again, seeding
elegies inside of them. Knowing they will pincushion

inside the urgent care's halogen as you uncork another.
They may not trust any man for years, even themselves
in their fogged bathroom mirrors, watching

as the shower fills space with thought. Especially
themselves. The doctor strung my elegy out
first thing Friday morning, let the blood and promised

he would call Tuesday, maybe Monday. He fed me
a rattling pill-bottle cap, filled a paper bag
for twenty-eight days. *Queer penance*, I joked outside

to the palms frocking the bus stop. But it wasn't
penance—it wasn't even queer. It was surviving
your vanishing condom, your vanishing

test results, one lie after the next. Surviving
your low house—rhododendrons oblivious
and furious to one side, blossoms shuddering

the highway below. No cars but a white panel
bakery truck. Does the yard's streetlight still shine
that bed new-penny copper each night? Do moths

gather around the story and lick? Do you ever check?

emet ezell
Has Your Spirit Dried Up?

darts and divots—wild javelina in the pit.
he tusks the grass when it rains, clumping up

mud and dirt. most people hate javelina: they are looking
for a guru, for a god. but here is

pig. hello pig! pig is perennial and
covered in hair. prickly pear cactus

blooms on his back. yellow petals. blood and
honey. pig bolts across field. pig is

bird without wings. most people want
to be lied to.

my mommy loves me.
sometimes my homeland is pig.

Kent Leatham

America's Last Hometown

> *"The less there is to justify a traditional custom,*
> *the harder it is to get rid of it"*
> —Mark Twain, *The Adventures of Tom Sawyer*

> *"no moral lesson could be drawn"*
> —John Steinbeck, *Tortilla Flat*

The house across the street is white.
I mean, the house across the street is white
as bleached sugar. I mean the house

across the street is white as sugar which has undergone
a refining process to remove all molasses.
I mean the sugar has undergone a process in which

bone char was used as a decolorizing agent.
I mean the sugar is white because of being
subjected to the blackened bones of livestock.

I mean cattle and pigs. I mean except for
the skulls and spines, which are no longer used
so as to avoid Creutzfeldt–Jakob disease.

I mean Mad Cow disease. I mean prions.
I mean in 2008, when the FDA banned
donated sperm for artificial insemination

from foreign countries so as to avoid
contamination. I mean countries in Europe.
I mean white on white. I mean I myself

am the donated child of a white stranger.
I mean the walls, doors, shutters, trim,
mailbox, fence. I mean my town is twenty miles

from Spreckels, home to the world's largest
sugar-beet refinery in 1899. I mean Claus Spreckels,
German immigrant and sugar baron,

who built and self-named the company town
twenty-one years after doing the same
with Spreckelsville, Hawai'i. I mean my father

could have lived across the street.
I mean as a child my mother took me
to Spreckels each year on the Fourth of July

to wave a flag and eat charred beef.
I mean my town was a Methodist retreat.
I mean we were white. I mean we red-lined.

I mean our Chinese fishing district
"mysteriously" burned down in 1906.
I mean we weren't the first people here.

I mean John Ernst Steinbeck spent half his childhood
three blocks away, and worked as a teen
in Spreckels' beet fields and factory labs.

I mean Mad Cow is fatal: the symptoms
include hallucinations, dementia, psychosis,
loss of coordination, spasms, pain.

I mean refining sugar removes calcium,
potassium, magnesium, iron. I mean the bones
are heated to 1,292 degrees. I mean

the byproduct not used for char is known
as Dippel's oil, after Johann Konrad Dippel,
an alchemist born at Castle Frankenstein

who published under the pseudonym
"Christianus Demócritus." I mean Dippel's oil
was used in World War II to foul

enemy wells in the Desert Campaigns.
I mean I too was a drop in a well.
I mean I too am an artificial grain.

I mean this town is in my bones.
I mean the house across the street
is "a steal at only $2.5 mil," is

"white, sweet, and yours to keep."

Sam Bailey
Why I'm a Xtian

It's about loneliness like a flower that explodes in your face when you go down to kiss it. That's what it's about. I don't make rules. It's about the trucker hat with the netting in the back like a bunch of gnats got sucked there by a magnet. It's about the sun breaking its one fucking rule. It's about the recycling bins blue as spring. It's about the bones in us, sweetheart. It's about the way you walk down the street observing these things and thinking your life is halfway over, twice, and is that the smell of rhubarb? Sure. And that's the smell of everything else in the world that says it won't harm you. It likes it, not harming you, everything else. Paul, I've forgotten you. But I haven't forgotten what it's about. I pocket the Gospel of Barnabas. It's about bicycles all jacked up by the sidewalk. About the bulls tattooed on the sidewalk. The lessons of puberty. It's about egoism, undone, forever. It's about cars that drive by me on a mission they won't speak about. I know their mission. Who gave it. Poetry, I need you to close your eyes for a second. Paul, now it's just us. When we get pulled past the Event Horzion, our bodies will still be here, walking around Ellsworth Street. They'll do things like push strollers and give hugs. But we will be off like sparrows woke up in Wite-Out or an LAX plane that never came back from the sun. Paul, that's actually not what's it about. What's it about, being invisible, is apricots on a Sunday in your grandmother's backyard where the sparrows peck around for other apricots and come up broke. It's about the text. About neo-criticism, which gets you here and only here and everywhere else in the sunshine. John Ashbery, go home stop reading this. Paul Sorrento of the Anaheim Angels: Stay. And now that truly everyone's gone, I would like to take my vows and admit something to you, with kindness. Or let's just do this. Get out the bullets. Roll them in your palm. They're joking. They're not. They're bigger than you. These shiny bronze ones that somehow in the light seem pink.

Cate Lycurgus

Martingale

> "It is sheer good fortune to miss somebody long before they leave you."
> —Toni Morrison, *Sula*

Long before I leave, I miss. Which is sheer
good fortune—: somebody stirs in the house,

in the body's good house, some fortune stirs
with each reel back from extinction—was dream

real? From each extinction, back to the dream
in its workaday shape, I rise blind—no,

I raise blinds; know it's days' work, as shapes
shift, to hold one. Lightly. Mostly I've had

to shift those I've held to *had*—most lightly
you press my shoulder—there's coffee waiting—

coffee you've pressed holds me—I wait there
to swallow, its scald will scorch my throat surely

scorched, my throat will swallow all—too sure
before long, I leave. Which is sheer mistake—

Lindsay Li
悲怆五阶段 *(heritage study)*

denial is a punchline tossed and crumpled as soda cans
and punched tickets. we girls avert our gazes

from the drifting eyes of self-portraits, untethered
from the peachy expanses of our faces. even the knights

our parents sent galloping through our hometowns to save us
become punchlines in the mouths of party drunks: chinks

in the armor. like white-sailed boats wandering
at sea, our gazes catch the afternoon sun and burn.

we are angry that we are not sons. not worshiped,
not the children our fathers wanted

to embrace from motherly wombs. and our mothers, themselves
children their own fathers tossed away—our mothers

dolled us in silk and paper, brushed our pupils with ink, pulled
our hair into fresh noodles, taught us the ways to condense

our feelings into downcast eyes, modest smiles. we bargained for gold
with our bodies. we gilded our eyes with brass for men

to pick and choose, our bodies purer than glass
figures: refracting every skewer of light, waiting

for husky time-whispered promises: *you're*
beautiful, have my children. every step reminds us

we don't exist to serve ourselves: fertilization, gestation, birth
of a girl for the cycle. our transparency remains maternal,

threaded back to a mother who understands why girls are
irrational, why we don't see the world through downy eyes,

why we never needed to paint our vision in blue-greens. in time, we learn
the delicate art of compromise, grind down the jagged edges

where our teeth meet our tongues. one day
we'll reject our deities and gnaw our family temples

down to lacquerware, splinters sticking our gums until we spit them
back onto their graves. still, though, denial crosses

its legs on the train seats beside us on the trip home,
hands two tickets to the conductor

and waits for the punch.

悲怆五阶段 *can be interpreted as "five stages of sorrow."*

Genevieve Watson
Last Supper

Los Angeles, 2022

As autumn leaves fold in on themselves
      like paper cranes, my family holds
a homecoming—it's strange to call it

      a *homecoming* because the woman
at the head of the table has six days left
      to live. That night, the house is feverish

with moonlight. I find my eyes pulled in
      by the sliver of her shadow, disfigured
in its contortion, a crescent moon spilling

      across the satin tablecloth. By now, she has
forgotten how to cook & her children
      never learned, so they bring dishes

from the Chinese grocery store, try their best
      to recreate the nights they spent relishing
her *lo bo gao*. As the table becomes

      an altar, I hold a dry tangerine in my mouth
like a sentence I can't say, a sentence refusing
      to be spoken. As a child, I imagined the day

I would learn to coat tomatoes in sugar
      like she did. As a child, I imagined
death as a house in flames. But here, nobody says

a word. Plates pile around her
in delicate mountains. In the hallway, a watercolor
      sampan careens down a waterfall—even it makes

a muted splash. Somewhere down the street, this reunion
      is real. This house is not a temple, the leaves
hang heavy and green. In her paintings, the waterfalls

      freeze like faces. But here, obscured
by a mask, I no longer see the vowels take shape
      on her lips. The accent that raised me turns

foreign. When I touch her, I touch a ghost, the tenderness
      trembles her wet hair, loosing like tangled lace
between my fingers. In the end, a text will break

      through the early morning fog, saying *it was*
clean, sterile and white. My family marks
      the morning on a calendar with red ink

but I saw her death before she even died—
      that night, through the eye
of the golden doorknob, I watched like a god.

Elizabeth Loudon
Renunciation

The clock on the waiting-room wall
is broken, the children mute with uncertainty
as they push wooden balls on a track,
tackety-tack. The lawyers told me to keep
my answers short. When my number comes up
I stand before bullet-proof glass
and count out words like small change.
A year ago. One daughter. Because I need
to simplify my life. The first time I became
American at heart a woman in piney woods
lifted her shirt over her head, singing Puccini.
The second time, the car flung sideways.
I had time while we spun to imagine
all kinds of worst. Snowplows came
to scrape us free and a stranger with sober eyes
gave us sweet tea. *Nobody made me.*
By train, last night, by myself, and with one scrawl
I'm forever no longer yours to whom
I gave my only begotten, I've no say left,
here where no time shows it's time go.
At the Embassy gate, guards shift guns
from left to right, signatures of heft.
My longer answers are folded unsigned
inside my pocket. I fell in love
with the man who walked over ice
to help us, he said nobody could blame bad weather,
in future accidents he might even walk on water.

Moment upon moment we continued
to live, to forgive, it was never the last time yet,
nothing was taken that couldn't be replaced.
Each time you lifted your hand, you promised.

Courtney DuChene
On Culling

My father scrapes zebra mussels
       from the hull of his boat.
             They're invasive, so he

          cleaves their shells in two
      using his fingernail, feeds flesh
to a frenzied family of ducks.

Empty carapaces butterfly-wing
      the shore. Last year, they clogged an
         intake pipe and the faucet gasped.

         Zebra mussels, male and female,
      release their eggs and sperm
to the water. When they meet, larva forms

and drifts away without considering
      questions of lineage. My mother
         wants to know if I'll have a baby

         and will I raise her here?
      She's become obsessed with family
history. Swabbing her mouth, spreading photos

on the dining room table,
      trying to trace a path back. Born
         under Capricorn, my mother clings

to December air: pine and festive wine.
When she sees a field of soybeans crippled
by heat, she says, *they need space to grow.* She mentions

a shuttered amusement park in Berlin
where weeds overtook rides. Tendrils grasped
roller coaster tracks. The mussel pile grows

at my father's feet. Here, by the river
poisoned with RoundUp and flushed Oxy.
Quietly, like a weakness, he says,

sometimes I think I see your sister
in the water, but when I look again,
it's just me. I say nothing, blame the heat.

Part goat, part fish, Capricorn
uses her hooves to drag her tail
to water, though she's lost her gills.

At supper, my mother and father talk of rain,
this drought-filled summer, how it sounds
impatient, fingers tapping on a table.

Brittany Male
Case Study

The neck of the desk lamp curved as though struck
into giving off its warm light. It is late.
I study to isolate the genomic variation
that makes the women of my lineage
undeserving of man's honesty.

A simple exploration into the sociological implications
of gender exposes the ongoing debate of a woman's choice.
I did not read on. A woman of my family knows to choose.
She must choose between her man's hands on another body in love
or on her own in anger.

But the research has no anthropological explanation
for every generation of women folding back into the one before
When they try to get their husbands out from another's bed.
They write letters through the night and slip them under doors
of separate bedrooms and separate houses. I've seen this all before.

And within them a different biological clock ticks,
their skin stretching tight over bones in time
because their lips touch nothing but questions.
Which part of what you've done scares you the most?
Which body is your magnum opus?

When they die, because they always do,
and they never think we're going to,
their notes are still there, in books given to grandchildren

and boxes sorted through by sisters.
Sentences abandoned halfway through,
timelines with pushpin-holes as though they came down
from an overpriced PI's investigation board,
extrapolated fears that they cannot tell
if they were crazy to believe.

My primary sources hold open one eyelid
and my academic research the other.
I taste their questions for the first time.
I wipe the vomit from my mouth.

Justin Rigamonti
Failure

The bee wasn't broken.
Just dying. Just turning circles
in the sand like it was missing
a wheel. Like it was trying to
get somewhere over and over
and failing. Because to truly fail
you must first try very hard.
The geometry of failure is always
inspirational at first: the thrill of it,
trying to catch your breath when
you can't quite. Aunt Diane said
watching you die was like
watching someone reach for a rope,
over and over, missing every time.
The long breath you needed
was a few inches too far.
As for the bee, I couldn't say
what it was reaching for.
One old drone far from its hive,
an insignificant loss. But for the drone,
the loss was total. Everything
must go: body, self, every dirty
grain of sand. I lifted the bee
from its sad carousel and set it
on the log where it died, and that act—
neither kind nor good—was what
I would have done for you:

lift your eyes to where they
tracked mine, where I knew
you could hear me.
But I was miles away. You
understood what was killing you,
the only way in which you were better
off than the bee. Your body
skeletal and heaving. I would have
laid my hand on your chest
and told you what you couldn't hear:
to stay alive isn't success.
And this isn't failure.

—Nominated by *Frontier Poetry*

Brian Czyzyk
Equinox

Now, the blades of leaves divide
the shadows on the forest floor

into split hearts. The wind makes a riot
of cold. March slips on green

socks, and somewhere a raccoon
grips a spear of grass in its muzzle

to make it whistle. Floorboards yawn.
A sapphire chips out of a robin's egg,

and this is how change arrives.
At its most expected, there is still

a shock of blood where a girl flattens
her knees against the trashed riverbank.

Her ribs cradle more breath than sound,
her hands grab at a downpour

of maple seeds, and she aims her ankles
at a noon-flushed cul-de-sac. She names

that place *memory of toothache*
and bramble-scratch, a kink at the back

of the throat, duskless and gray-puddled
and hollow as dovesong. She slides

a spiral shell from the brass chain
around her neck and watches her trail

bend in the sand, away from the water,
away from the woods, her steps unmasking

shoots arranged like points on a crown.

Mckendy Fils-Aimé
the lougawou discusses repetition

it is not enough to repeat a word
until it loses meaning. say it more.
again. say it until your teeth wear away

the tips & corners of the letters. the spelling
more comical than concerning. say it like a slur
a tired printer slips onto a sheet of paper,

like there isn't meaning under the smudge.
let's practice: *LOUGAWOU, lougAWOU, lougawou.*

in the courtyards of port-au-prince, the kids chant
my name, hurl it like pebbles at an old man
when he scolds them for stealing

his mangoes. now lougawou is no longer
nightmarish, amorphous, but a synonym
for levity. now when one of those kids breaks

into a fever, his parents might say malaria
before my name. once, a mob would have
marched to the old man's home & hung him

in search of a cure. once, they would have
looked at every elder like a fountain of wisdom
teeming with puffer fish. once, i would have feared

slipping into their homes, shadow-sprawling
across their children's rooms, swallowing
tiny beds. my dark blending into the dark.

my maw eager to drink their babies
breathless. now i barely remember thirst,
famine a dead language

in the history of my stomach. & all i had
to do was lend them my name, let them whisper it
like an omen, lighter after each retelling, weightless

like a good joke. my name a punchline
& the laughter it ushers. my name fangless
as a boa slowly coiling around your throat

Jackie Sabbagh

Having a Great Time Being Transgender in America Lately

It is day infinity
of everyone wanting me dead. People are having fun
bringing lemon squares and automatic artillery to the anti-trans community meetings.
Divorced legislators harangue
about pedophile cults and surgeried infants and whatever happened to forever ago.
I am more beautiful than you, and I would like to be loved.
And I'm getting concerned
about the monomaniacs who make their entire lives about deadnaming and transvestigations—
obviously it's working but aren't you exhausted, don't you remember
when someone loved you without knowing what you were?
I am eating shortbread on a patio table overlooking the enormous green ocean.
Somewhere an octopus is being eaten by an octopus and not panicking.
Black dress to the floor, red acrylic nails, silver teardrop earrings, waterproof mascara.
I am excited to do this the rest of my life and be terrified.
I hear a noise behind me, and I don't turn around.

Sophie Pedersen

feast on your life

after derek walcott

at a nightclub in thailand
a mauritian ICU doctor
tells me he once extracted
a set of salt and pepper shakers
from his patient's asshole
the guy claimed he tripped and fell
on the kitchen floor
there's two inches of separation
arshad says
between the right kind of pleasure
and the kind you lie about
until it kills you
afterward arshad and schesley
take turns licking my pussy folds
they've known each other
since middle school
since the island days
since before creole
was a written language
just soft sounds
in the gums of a mouth
in the morning
we eat slabs of coconut
pork belly with bubbly skin
sticky rice in thick milk
we take pictures of the oldest tree
on the island

for 400 years
it's been watching people fuck and eat
and tell stories about it
at the foot of it
someone laid a shrine
of buddhas and marigolds
i wonder if the tree
is choosing to live
or living against its will
and which version of the story
people think they're worshipping
at the beach rave
half naked hippies
open their organs
up to the beat
and for two whole songs
we pretend we're not terrified
of our own bodies
and their rank desires
arshad asks about my meds
he says i'm lucky
he once treated someone
who has what i have
she stabbed herself in the heart
with a kitchen knife
i tell him i used to fantasize
about something serrated
entering my lungs
fuck
he says
you wanna do lines?
we buy coke from the california man

and motorbike home
arshad yells something into the wind
it sounds like
i'm glad you're alive
but it also could've been
let's fuck all night
either way it's extremely romantic
and i press my cheek into his back
he speeds up
and makes a sharp turn
our bodies lean parallel
to the potholes
i reach under his armpits
and finger the hair on his shoulder blades
i cling on and then i cling on harder
i got the will to live
i think
for centuries

Mary Spooner
Here in My Unincorporated Plot

I fashion a man from plastic
with rubber boots and spurs.

His arm goes all the way around
in its socket. His hat never falls off.

I tell him: I've been a woman
folded down the center.

I've been a glass of beer.
I hold my fingers and thumb

like a pistol between my legs.
What do you make of this?

He says: Admit
you have grown tired of your exile,

have wanted both property
and deliverance from property,

a vista so open
you could outwalk yourself.

Do not lie, I say. I made you
so I could practice loving you.

You made me so
you can take my boots off.

You take them off
to put them on again.

Michael Hurley

Vespers or Orison or Haven

Don't you remember when
we found the dead pumpkins
glowing in the field—fire
in the snow, and shining,
the fire was shining, sun dipping
down while still each little
brittle fire was shining, because
each was cased in ice.

Ice, for ice, for cold
sharpened to a shard
or flattened to a shield,
to a film that forms over
each contour like a peel,
a shell of cold made by cold,
a borrowed thickness
to guard against the wind.

And our visiting friend peeled them
careful as oranges, large halves intact,
then rebuilt them on a branch, then he took
a picture of each, little empty
crystal urns. We left him to it,
came back later. It seemed then
and now to be some sort
of quiet grace or grief and when
the sun rose back up

and the warmth made them crack,
they made secret noises
as they broke, little tinks.

D. M. Spratley
The Collector of Debts

Though she's been gone two years now, these people still dig up my mother's name
from their mounds of debt to be collected. The payday loan rep is persistent

as mint in a garden—as in, *You must be her daughter*. I say, *You are speaking to her ghost,*
because it makes him stutter. No doubt he pictures my mother smirking into the phone.

(Inside me, a haint bubbles with laughter. We are neither of us wrong.)
The haint and I sit on the couch and cradle the dog, his hot breath rising and his belly

hoping the ceiling will reach down to pet it. We've set the phone aside and the lender
crackles through, his mouth a loop of ecstatic tongues, a list of things we no longer own

and which he says he plans to take from us. *What else*, we purr, *once the house is gone?*
so that his voice grows dull with spit and shame. The haint and I pat the dog's head

delightedly, with the selfsame hand. Yes—let's call us one—
for when the haint crossed the threshold of this home in spite of the sage I burned,

the garlic anchored in every doorway, every eye open to the world, she fit
herself inside me. (Perfect fit. Hand in glove.)

So when she pats the head of the dog, he sways like a dancer, giddy from our touch.
When she feeds him, he tumbles at our feet and asks for more.

When she lowers my soul into the well of sleep, he lies beside our body,
and he doesn't dream of her sins, and she doesn't dream at all, and I dream

that she shouts my name from the bottom of an impossible gorge, the bottom noisy
and inscrutable with chatter. She tells me to throw a rope down into the din, for her escape

from the land of the dead. (Where I could get pulled in.) (And when she calls, I answer.)

Alejandro Lucero

When I search "Sapello,"

for Carlos Martinez, who discovered and named the Sapello asteroid

you and your asteroid pop
up above news of the latest wildfire.

I recognize the jelled bristles and shadow
of your widow's peak, ignore the report of ash seeping into the water supply

from which I no longer drink. Carlos, the box cutter kid,
you grew up between grocery aisles, stocking Little Debbies

at your dad's store. Why did you name that shrinking stone,
stripped by atmosphere, after our hometown? Why not

your mother? Hell, why not the red beads of the pigweed's
wind-stripped vine? Those flowers our ancestors picked

off their socks—private gardens between the boot
and hem. I name my torn-up sneakers *Sapello*

shit kickers. Give friends with one last chance the last name
(Sapello) in my address book. Driving home blackout drunk

is *calling a Sapello taxi*. Where we're from they trick calabacitas
from the brittle dirt with river water, plant framed photos

next to homemade graves. You chose to burn your eyes
with calculus, soothe them against the cool glass of research

-grade telescopes. Professor Martinez,
teach me about the joys of being a child in Sapello

obsessed with night. Did you butterfly a sleeping bag
each weekend, waiting for shooting stars? Collect crickets

in Coke cans for their company, their music? Professor, tell me
you rattled them, your makeshift mariachi band,

when you nodded off below that tapestry of stars.
I picture you as a boy gazing black holes into the galaxy,

safe from the cries of starved coyotes. Someone's chained-up
mutts shouting back across the field. Tufts of Russian thistle

we call tumbleweeds stuck in the small teeth
of your barbed wire fence. I want to find that old article

with a photo of my childhood home beneath the title, an iris of fire
rising in the background. Would you have refused the evacuation

orders, exercised your right to sit back and choke on the smoke of ponderosa
pines? I never felt the warmth of a fireplace. My Sapello was blown

pilot lights. My family too afraid to light a match
in the winter drought. The wind turned our trailer into a frozen harmonica.

When you first saw it move, yellow tail stretched like a sentence,
the name was ready on your tongue. Your little Sapello

burning across our cracked leather sky.

Acie Clark

Self-Portrait as Orpheus on T

The dog no longer recognizes my voice.
At the window, I call his given name.
Spoken to, he runs in circles, looks up
to the sound but can't see me through the glass.
That, or he no longer recognizes my face, either.
I can see my face now in the window, mirrored back.
Sometimes it takes me a second to remember:
I gave up my forever face for this new one.
I wanted to feel right. To align out with within.
To get inside of the word *who*, to feel, I *am*.
Under my eye's constant photography,
I look for traces of the forever-I. Once, I looked
at my face for the last time. I wanted to. I saw
nothing changed. Becoming was how I was
right there when I turned me around.
I selfed a little. I felt self-ish, so I selfed a little more.
I can start to stop but I can't start over.
My forever face softens in reverse photography.
When I touch the picture, my hands lift
from the puddle of a window still reflecting
our face. In the right light, glass jumps out
and back into its frame. Not all mirrors mean to
mirror. These eyes have always been my eyes.
The dog is inside now, looking out,
searching for whoever it is I see there.

Mason Wray
After Birds

In Warsaw, they've translated
the former Communist headquarters
into a shot bar.

We sip Sobieski out back
where officials went to say
what they couldn't inside

for fear of being understood

by the wrong people.
How to explain,

Oleg muses
as he translates
Polish idioms:

What does gingerbread have to do with a windmill?

Not my circus, not my monkeys.

After birds

is what you say when
something's over for good.

One-fourth of white storks
left on earth
summer in Poland

though fewer return each year.

The truth about storks is
they can't speak
even to each other.

That they deliver babies
is the misunderstanding
of an ancient Greek myth

about cranes.

This reminds me of Sara's geriatric neighbor
who planted a giant plywood stork
in her tomatoes to scare sparrows

then spent all summer accepting
anonymous diaper donations.

Fear of being misunderstood
is called ambiguphobia.

When Jimmy Carter visited Warsaw in '77,
the specter of the bomb
hung incessantly overhead
like mistletoe at an office party.

He spoke cautiously of his hope
to improve international relations.

In Polish it came out as
a desire to grasp
the country's private parts.

Around us, deep house techno
ricochets off the facade
of a fallen government.

I'm afraid I'll only understand

something's over for good
once it's gone.

Nearby a stork
translates utility pole
into nest.

Laura Cresté
Between 5,000 and 12,000 Years After the Eruption

We lower into the cave system as a bucket
into a well. Cows lowing over our heads.

The water from the ceiling runs clean.
If this was your country, the guide explains,

the stalactites would grow long,
minerals building out. But this water is pure.

The ancient ceiling stipples with short nubs,
pips of cream on the edge of a cake.

I think of nipples and cows carting their milk
all over the island. I have to think more of myself

in this language. Thank you invokes gender, not
of the thanked but the thanker. I, a woman, thank you,

I say all day long. It is one of several words I know.
That and the menu sectioning up the cow.

How to say I'll take the milk but not the meat.
Give me the leather without the harm.

I want the marriage without property.
This, our life, without an end.

Jonathan Diaz

Your Old Men Shall Dream Dreams, Your Young Men Shall See Visions

There was a dispute over the inheritance,
you would tell me as I swung
in the woven hammock, watching
the breeze brush over your garden.

So many hectares to your father, so many
to each of your uncles. Some relatives
grumbled over their allotment and
enviously eyed the plot you tended.

One night, the Holy Spirit woke you
in time to see your cousin creeping
into your room, his machete raised
above his head. When he parted

the mosquito net, you pulled the pistol
from your breast pocket and pointed
it, silently, at him. Always, you told me,
I must be prepared to hear God speak.

I have tried to be vigilant, but no
voice has yet called me in the night.
Is it any wonder I sleep fitfully,
some heavy, lethal thing against my heart?

—Nominated by *Beloit Poetry Journal*

Rachel Rothenberg
Blessings over the Bodies of My Father's Murderers

May your mothers find you whole. May the sky hold
your bodies unbroken as the light before the flood.

May our makers never demand we row out
beyond the deluge. May their every promise

hold. May moonlight replace the flash and howl
of the alarms. May the water tenders sluice the fires

to mud and mist before nightfall, may the switchboard
hold the calls. May the cranes hollow their burrows

in the wet earth, may their hooks graze the loose
fists of your ribcage. May they lift your fingers

gentle as the hands of your mothers. May the coroners
recover the horned rungs of your vertebrae whole

and not scattered here in the oil slick, buried
there in the singed grasslands. May they ladder you

away like the strands of DNA helixed to arrest
dissolution, may they wind you back to your separate

bodies. May the dome of heaven refit the arced
continents of your skulls, may your bones find their way

out of evidence. May your mothers slack your hold
may they gather your knuckles loosed from the tusk

handles and bury your knives clean. May you unslash
his throat. May your mothers cut you from this earth

whole. May we wake to any given morning anywhere
but here in this burning field, extinguished and whole.

—Nominated by *Shenandoah*

Shelly Stewart Cato
River, Heron, Doe

When I'd faced the heron earlier

on my paddleboard, I hadn't seen

she was broken, standing there unmoving.

I thought I'd developed a power,

a hypnotic charge, a way to brim time. Then,

like a vent in the forest-scape,

a deer beside her fanned out cattails and began

drinking. Three bodies—mine, the heron, the doe—

and the current glided my board so that, at one point,

it was as if I were looking through

the heron's silhouette to the bronzed deer behind her—

three points in perfect alignment.

An eclipse. And then she flustered

her left wing—only her left—and the deer vanished

into this lush and spellbound river game.

That's when I saw her wing, hackneyed, the inner vane,

blood-pink. Game over. River,

after night-drop, you will grasp this heron by the ankles,

swoosh her pillowed head

through marsh grass and drag her down, down,

her perfect wing still tremoring.

And then, River, you will suck the bird's throat down your throat

and the tarnished darter in her gullet still swimming.

You win, River. River beats rock, holed

and hollowed sand ledges breaching the air above.

River beats lipped-up whitecaps, curling to ash. And in the morning,

you will hawk up her lavender feathers

creweled with hyacinth root and diesel.

Letitia Chan
Inheritance

Finished with the world my father returns to my mother,
like a car taking its final parking spot, as finished on the question
of love I move to Manchester to be with you. Bobblehead on
the dashboard vibrates its features off, an arctic blur, that's what
my love is like, a child tapping heels on a tricycle, trying. The wind
of you shattered me, making me hard to catch in frieze, in icing,
the limits to this love, its mouth performing the governing stitches
to say I'd follow you to the next place, say never leave me, in this town
lurid with its lights, where deer look back with haunted eyes. Heedless
of the weight of life, I know a way to make it last, to stretch the minutes
of sherbet, the ticking bomb inside a body, the other left behind.
I want to move you, as I wanted to move my father, who could never
be impressed, as I wanted to move my mother, who could never be
impressed upon, two disparate figures made of water they were,
rippling, a movement getting lost in the larger reverb of the lake
which absorbed the minutiae of their lives, in my limited webbing
the child in me grown jowls, grown into sounds of creaking, of
creakage, there were days left, and only days, and only all of us taking
our sadnesses by their wayside and their last hairs and their curtains
and turning over in a new sleep about it. I can't bear you holding
all your pain alone. I see you getting small and bright and your face
fisted and tight-pinched with it, when your attention's caught by
something you find beautiful, the times you think I'm not looking,
didn't notice the earth around you was becoming rearranged as
when the tectonics placed you somewhere new and unmappable,
the way you looked, forlorn as a duckling, filled me with water, and I
thought this is what every parent leaves their child, every lover

the beloved, grief, induced it how, the heart hollowed with fireside,
the wrong sights, the mistakes on which I had made a life very far
from everything I wanted to keep at bay, how they shone as
composite and discrete marbles, and, jewelling, glimmered on.

—Nominated by The New York University Creative Writing Program

Katey Funderburgh
Dinner Party

The evening light formed another
birthmark on my arm and you said
I was a good host. The closest I have
ever come to permanence is the window
in my kitchen where I watch
the trees and their shadows, where
I stir the pasta and think about you.
Last night's bourbon was sweeter
than I expected and so was
the bread, the fish, the tiramisu.
So was your hand on my forearm.
I learned to use a gun when I was small,
just in case, and in nightmares
I wade through all of your bones. Last
night, my chest was the shape of yours.
I measured it again this morning, just
in case, and it still is. Each plate washed
is a body fed so please don't ever die.
Can you see I am trying to be gentle with
myself? I am trying to feed the good monster,
not the one who is afraid of dying last
but the one who knows about portions of salt
and tupperware containers and constelled freckles
and the small music of the wind chime hung
over my front door. Please come in, sit next to me.
You already know that the first leaf to yellow
is also the first to fall. There are so many

wars—I love you, just in case. I am so bad
at singing. There are so many ways
to hate yourself, please
pass your glass to me, I've opened
another bottle. We are hungry because
god is real. We are thirsty because
god is not. I would hurt
someone who hurt you and
I'm sorry. Here, stay. Let me
see you listen when I say that I
forgive myself because the world is ending, and
I forgive the world because you're here.

G.H. Plaag
Televised

we are all in one room, drinking
cocktails mixed with legacy brand
liquors. we don't notice. we forget
that companies are responsible
for our vodka, for our water, for
our lights and for our roads, we forget
but we remember, too. we talk
about our reading lists, a girl is
reading *Agua Viva*, she says
Lispector had a way to see
around the bend of time, she hits
a vape beneath a sky that glows
the bronze of fresh-stripped wire.
soon a Beyoncé song comes on inside
the purple bar, which nudges us
to bitch about the ethics of our billionaires,
and then to dance. we run the world.
we are also the resistance. we sew
red patches with thread from Jo-Ann Fabrics.
thanks, Jo-Ann. we love you Jo-Ann.
we love you Tito. we love you
Ralph Lauren. we love you
and we are never going to be
quiet, you'll never hear our voices
fall silent. we are plotting
your demise, we are architecting
better worlds, we are watching

how you scissor us in half.
we are young but we will live
beyond you. we grip our city
with arms and hands made fast
by all your evil tools. we are posting this
to TikTok so the Chinese government knows
that we are hot and young and slutty
in our artificial cages, in our handcuffs,
in our straps. we need the spies
to learn about femdom and
the Wednesday Dance. we know,
we know—this could threaten everything
that makes this country great, our security
could be at risk, but we don't care. we don't believe
in borders or in anything. you have taken that
from us, belief. and you only have
yourselves to blame. we are all
in one room and we are angry,
we are vicious, we are tired, we are
trying to find a way home. we are all in
one room, and the room is everywhere
in distance of a cell tower, everywhere
our ankle monitors can beep. we can't
get out and we're becoming feral, we are starving,
we're exhausted, we are pretty, we are desperate,
we are entertained, we're young and we are dangerous,
we are all in one room. we know damn well
who put us here. and when we make it out,
teeth gnashing, eyes alight with fear
and hope, we'll be like any uncaged thing:
we'll kill before we go back in.

—Nominated by *ANMLY*

Alexander Lee
Memorial Day & How We Fight

We feast on silence, my brother and I, eyes gobbling up
each flash across our phone screens. Chopsticks

criss-cross—a habit since birth for us, one
we never bothered to change. The wooden

chopsticks scratch against each other, hiss angrily, crackle

the smoked seaweed like dried campfire kindling. Lost
in summer's technicolor sea, I was oblivious to knuckles

whitened by chopsticks, the translucent plastic cup's hard-set
lip. The mindless bombs of roe flowed over

my three stories of kimbap. As each one panged
inside my mouth, each bursting red shell fired

without a sound. After lunch, he walked up to me. *Say
you're sorry.* My voice rang sharply—*For what?* I'd said

fuck off. You're not my mom, after he told me to stop
scarfing spicy pickles. *Say you're sorry*—he waited for me

to succumb to his headlock. I didn't—though
like a shock of peonies to the face, I couldn't

breathe—knots of anger loomed in my eyes. Dad blurred
in narrowed sight, wrestling him away. Kneeling, as if

honoring the fallen, I reached for my phone, a birthday gift
from my brother—a gift that had skipped

across the kitchen floor, scratching the tiles as it went.

Kate DeLay
Repair

I hear my calf braying into the indigo under
half-faced moons, a slurry of sight & sound. On these nights,
the calf & I stand shoulder to shoulder at the fence
of the world, our sorrow weeding
the pasture behind us, that soybean-sucked soil, leeched & lingering.

& the barbed wire hums into the grasses: & the blue light bends
around our bodies: & our fingernails are caked with fight.
The world calls out to us, wet & wanting.
            O field, I tried to leave you
& never be left. I longed to lift the electric
fence & free my calf from the field, our leaving
a plucked string for the night choir.

But for the fight of that field, I met the calf.
& when I share her eyes, she sees stars. I carry her
earth in my earth, find a field in every fold. My shadow bends
around me like four new legs, stitched from a
womb of nightshade & dew.

& I made a home in the world. & everywhere, the world loves itself
in me. When I remember that field, I listen
softly. When I love that field, I sing.

Chi Pham
Italian Lambskin Leather Gloves

The lamb in the dream
was not a lamb. But a child.

Its cries were wet, like a knife through cartilage
or humid night air. I shot it twice;

it would not die. My father's hands, how precise
those instruments, taught me how to hold the gun.

His voice is a metronome against my ear: *Wait. Wait.
Not yet. Wait.* Leather soles on wooden stairs,

counting each step upward like a rosary—
the only prayer I learned by ear alone. *Mercy*—

a word I learned to use differently in our house.
How *merciful* the stray bullet. How *merciful*

each stroke striking the body. How merciful
the woman in leather gloves who serves the meat

without looking at what she touches. This is discipline:
to hold the wanting until it changes shape.

No one's too good to forgive. You aren't.
Father's the exception. His belt slides through loops

with the sound of something
leaving. *Come on—*

One last exertion. One last act that leads nowhere
but to the fist of childhood, clenched around

its own weightlessness like a bal-
loon fired. *Blessing*

the small death that follows antici-
pation. *Blessing*

the pause before surrender. Say it:
Blessing. The way your body obeys before

your mind decides. The way desire pools
in the sheath around command and sacrifice. The way

it feels to be killed, and just before witness arrives,
your soul snaps back in place like ammunition

returned to its chamber. At dawn,
the lamb's alive again, guts glistening

with resurrection's wet. I fire. I miss.
I fire. Between intention and bruise is where

God likes to make Himself felt, watching us fumble
with our fathers' weapons, returning us

to the moment right before release. When I wake,
the lamb's crying still. I hear it in the wind,

the creak of my bedroom door. The Italian
leather gloves, folded on the mantle,

hold the shape of what won't come:
mercy that arrives before we learn to ask for it.

Immaculate, rotten symmetry.

Tobi Kassim
Heavyweight

I know hard things have
their yielding places. I've seen
the fabricator lean into the raw

edge of slabbed earth with the weight
of his hip while his Makita hummed
like a record. He swayed in time

with reggaeton off the shop radio, side
to side for friction like he found a dance
partner in stone. I press the heel of my palm

against my eyelids and see blood
veined across a century's smooth
face. Weight of every day compacted in it.

We removed a mountaintop to reach
stone's deep refuge. Weight of deep
belonging. Used clamps to brace the slate's breaking

points on a metal frame. Water to absorb
debris's dispersal off sandpaper. Dust and mist
flew in the air like music. It took grace to force

the finer particles free—I press
my palm over my eyelids for dots of light
to dance in the dark of a hard question.

I feel the drag of granite's weight under
every day. Merril could polish a kitchen
in forty-five minutes. Why did we come back

to work and find him sprawled under
a morning's halo of beer cans? Leftover Bud
Light's sweetness mixed with dizzy whiffs

of mineral spirits to lift the final shine
out of the counters. The night got long
like that I guess. Some things never

have to end. He'd wake to ease back
onto the heavy machines. Cut kitchens
til sunup. Press the grit of stone edges

away with pleasure. There's no home like the glaze
over the world after I rub my eyelids
open to the uncollected softness of the dust.

A stone split breathes particulate
light, pipes the morning mist through
my pupils. The rest of the sun descends slowly

into gray puddles ankle-deep
on the shop floor. I guess tomorrow arrived
without the slightest rough patch in it.

Jen Siraganian
Thinking About My Father's Erector Set from 1948

Rarely my father speaks of the slow rubble piling,
before months sped hotter than his parents expected.
They thought it would pass, unaware of what aches
appear later. He was eight. This was before
walls, checkpoints, talk of two states.

Let's focus on one wound at a time. I can only tell
a story diluted. I'll try more softly—my father had toys,
then he didn't. He had a childhood, then he didn't.

Here is me at a sun-lit kitchen table in California,
doubling as American and something like coarse salt.

How often I hear it's *complicated* when I mention
my father grew up in Palestine, went to school in Palestine,
immigrated to the U.S. as a Palestinian refugee.

His voicemail last week—*don't post anything online.*

For years, he lived in no-man's land, and I,
half-Armenian, half-daughter of a man
from half of a land that is half of me.

When I visited, could I call the wall beautiful, but only
the painted side? My grandmother's friend spit on
for shopping on the wrong street in Jerusalem.
Jews walk on one, Muslims the other.
She's neither. *I started paying a man to do the errands.*

Seeing my father's childhood home, its walls
adorned with sniper fire and a gravity of collisions.
It consumed me, bullet holes as common as commas.

In the Armenian Quarter, the pottery store owner
said he would close before things worsened.
Palestine his home, until it wasn't. Truths stitched
into my grandmother's embroidery. Did I
tell you she left that too? Here is an echo
no one asked for, singing of a home
in Jerusalem before Armenians evaporated.

At the airport, I, though not yet vapor,
say nothing to the Israeli passport agent.
Not telling him I visited Palestine. Not asking
for the return of the toys my father left behind.

Melissa McKinstry

Late Spring Epiphany After the Georgia O'Keeffe Exhibit

I'm always trying to paint that door—
I never quite get it,
she said of the black square
at her winter house in Abiquiú,
always a shadow shifting,
a ladder leading to sky.
When she looked through
a pelvic bone she picked up
in the desert, she saw
a ghost moon,
and today I'm quiet
as her bones and stones
and black pearl oyster shells.
Once I had a son. Once,
when he was four,
before his tracheotomy,
we were invited to float
in a warm therapy pool.
He was weightless
as I swirled his thin limbs
in slow circles and lines.
He seemed to sleep
through it all, but I loved it:
his buoyancy, absence of straps
and wheels. Water flicker
on his curly lashes,
maybe a quiver of smile.

He couldn't say *more*,
or *mmmmm*, or *get me out of here*,
so I don't really know.
I never really knew him.
He kept himself to himself,
maybe grew very small
to survive. He was a dark door,
a box of bones—
a soft, gone tabernacle.

Benjamin Voigt
Grief

We kept our grief in a jar
under the sink. Dad collected it
there after we ate. It sweated
from the bacon like the bacon
was scared to be cooked.
I dreaded it: the rot
that filled the room
when the pickle-green cap
popped off.
Cooled, it thickened
into icing, layers of it
waiting with the rubber gloves
and old sponges
like a trifle. I still expect it
when I open
my own cabinet. We threw out
what we bottled up when we couldn't
bottle any more.
We were forbidden from pouring it
down the drain.
Years later, I'd read why,
about what happens
in sewers because
people do, our collective
grief congealing
beneath our streets
into icebergs

with human hair.
If it was still fresh,
we sometimes cooked with it
instead: its thick stink somehow
enriching whatever it slickened.
Down the hatch,
I would say to myself, funneling it
into my pipes, my own body
becoming the land
at the landfill
our grief was usually plowed into,
the grass growing
beside the plastic vents
on the lumpy hillsides
despite or because of
what we buried there.

—Nominated by *Cave Wall*

Lo Naylor
object permanence

the baby is trying to understand
when I hide behind the pillow, it doesn't mean
I'm gone for good.

there are other games like this.
she must wait for the ball
she slots in the chute

to drop into the box
at the bottom. this winter
they put my sister in a cardboard coffin

someone slid into an oven
& what came out
fit into a small box.

the day after she was found,
I left the baby for the first time.
I sat in an aluminum tube

barreling through the air
& landed next to the Great Salt Lake—
it wasn't illogical

to expect I'd find my sister there.
still, I refused to see her.
a friend said seeing the body can help you

accept the permanence of death—
yet breath can be so subtle,
I might have to use my hand or cheek to check.

back home, I go straight to the crib,
rest my palm on the tiny body inside—
a nearly imperceptible expansion.

a nearly unbearable expansion in me.
what is it?
the little fists punch the air.

the eyes open—a face
of disbelief on the return of mother.
how terrible

to be a creature that doesn't know
if the disappeared carry on out of sight,
may one day materialize—

Hannah Kosak
Portrait Returning to the Fog

Let me say more about this feeling—

cool mist unspools from the pines
like loose thread from an old dress
unstitching after a wash,

as a deer, stumbling drunkenly
out of the pointed wood and pausing,
breathless, ears pricked, in the road,

considering for a moment the sound
of oncoming traffic: the rush and hiss
of tires peeling away from asphalt,

the pebbles clattering into the shoulder
like a handful of dropped coins
lost between uneven floorboards,

decides, then, that it prefers
the shape and shadow of the trees,
and turning, melts back into the mist,

like a car pulling into a garage,
or a raindrop landing on,
then becoming, the sea.

—Nominated by The Writing Seminars at Johns Hopkins University

Acknowledgments

Sam Bailey's "Why I'm a Xtian" previously appeared in *The Adroit Journal*.

Shelly Stewart Cato's "River, Heron, Doe" previously appeared in *EcoTheo Review*.

James Ciano's "The Committee of Men (Haze)" previously appeared in *The Missouri Review*.

Acie Clark's "Self-Portrait as Orpheus on T" previously appeared in *Screen Door Review*.

Brian Czyzyk's "Equinox" previously appeared in *Tampa Review*.

Kate DeLay's "Repair" previously appeared in *The Adroit Journal*.

Jonathan Diaz's "Your Old Men Shall Dream Dreams, Your Young Men Shall See Visions" previously appeared in *Beloit Poetry Journal*.

Courtney DuChene's "On Culling" previously appeared in *New England Review*.

emet ezell's "Has Your Spirit Dried Up?" previously appeared in *Los Angeles Review of Books*.

José Felipe Ozuna's "Undocumented Sonnet" previously appeared in *Muzzle Magazine*.

Mckendy Fils-Aimé's "the lougawou discusses repetition" previously appeared in *The Adroit Journal*.

Harrison Hamm's "Ghost of a Peacock" previously appeared in *Susurrus*.

L. A. Johnson's "Birthmark" previously appeared in *The Atlantic*.

Tobi Kassim's "Heavyweight" previously appeared in *The Adroit Journal*.

Anya Kirshbaum's "Letter from the Edge of Every Known Thing" previously appeared in *SweetLit*.

Peter LaBerge's "California Avenue" previously appeared in *The Georgia Review*.

Alexander Lee's "Memorial Day & How We Fight" previously appeared in *The Tusculum Review*.

Janiru Liyanage's "The Deer" previously appeared in *32 Poems*.

Elizabeth Loudon's "Renunciation" previously appeared, in a slightly different form, in *Shō Poetry Journal*.

Alejandro Lucero's "When I search 'Sapello,'" previously appeared in *The Florida Review* and the chapbook *Sapello Son* (Bull City Press).

Melissa McKinstry's "Late Spring Epiphany After the Georgia O'Keeffe Exhibit" previously appeared in *The Adroit Journal*.

Lenna Mendoza's "You can't really *clean* the piercing gun at Claire's," previously appeared in *Salt Hill Journal*.

Brooke Middlebrook's "Après L'Ondée" previously appeared in *The Cincinnati Review*'s miCRo series.

Lo Naylor's "object permanence" previously appeared in *The Missouri Review*.

Jupiter Nesky's "Kiddush Levana" previously appeared in *Glass Poetry*.

G.H. Plaag's "Televised" previously appeared in *ANMLY*.

Dora Prieto's "Girls of the Now [Garments]" previously appeared in the 2025 Bronwen Wallace Award for Emerging Writers Anthology.

Justin Rigamonti's "Failure" previously appeared in *Frontier Poetry*.

Rachel Rothenberg's "Blessings over the Bodies of My Father's Murderers" previously appeared in *Shenandoah*.

Jackie Sabbagh's "Having a Great Time Being Transgender in America Lately" previously appeared in *Poetry*.

Jen Siraganian's "Thinking about My Father's Erector Set from 1948" previously appeared in *New Ohio Review*.

Mary Spooner's "Here in My Unincorporated Plot" previously appeared in *The Adroit Journal*.

D. M. Spratley's "The Collector of Debts" previously appeared in *The Adroit Journal*.

Nur Turkmani's "Animal Grief" previously appeared in *Poetry*.

Benjamin Voigt's "Grief" previously appeared in *Cave Wall*.

Genevieve Watson's "Last Supper" previously appeared in *The Adroit Journal*.

Mason Wray's "After Birds" previously appeared in *The Kenyon Review*.

Contributors' Notes

SAM BAILEY is from Central Pennsylvania. His poems are out or forthcoming in *The Yale Review*, *Image*, *Missouri Review*, *The Adroit Journal*, *Colorado Review*, and elsewhere. He's a PhD student in religion at Harvard University and serves as the associate editor of *Peripheries* and co-editor-in-chief of *Mark: A Journal of Christian Poets*.

JESSICA BOWDOIN is an English professor and Autistic poet in Austin. She received her MFA from the University of New Orleans. Recently, she was published in the twenty-fifth anniversary issue of *Smartish Pace* as a finalist for the 2024 Beullah Rose Poetry Prize and was selected for *Inverted Syntax*'s 2023 Sublingua Prize for Poetry. Her work can be found in *Best New Poets*, *Smartish Pace*, *Inverted Syntax*, *Ocean State Review*, *Beyond Queer Words* (2023), *Ellipsis*, and elsewhere. Connect with her on Instagram @jessica_bowdoin.

SHELLY STEWART CATO lived in the Mississippi Delta for twenty-five years and now writes and paints on Mulberry Fork in Walker County, Alabama. When she is on the river on her paddleboard, it is still on the river—sometimes—and there is peace. And she can see things she would never have seen before. She is passionate about genre-bending and experimenting with form, long poems and refrains, and blurring lines between truth and imagination. She is so thankful to *EcoTheo Collective* for first publishing "River, Heron, Doe." Connect with her on Instagram @shellyscato.

LETITIA CHAN is an MFA candidate and Writers in the Public Schools Fellow at New York University.

JAMES CIANO is the author of *The Committee of Men*, forthcoming from BOA Editions in April 2026. He holds an MFA from New York University and a PhD in creative writing and literature from the University of Southern California. His recent poems have appeared or are forthcoming in *The Southern Review*, *Bennington Review*, *The Hopkins Review*, and *The Yale Review*. His reviews and writings on poetry have appeared in *The Adroit Journal*, *Poetry Northwest*, and *Los Angeles Review of Books*. Under Editor David St. John, he is an associate editor of *Swirl & Vortex: Collected Poems of Larry Levis* (Graywolf Press, 2026). James is currently the 2025–2027 Creative Writing Fellow in Poetry at Emory University.

ACIE CLARK is a writer from Florida and Georgia. A former writing fellow at the Fine Arts Work Center in Provincetown, he teaches in the Film, Theatre, and Creative Writing Department at the University of Central Arkansas and as an instructor at Interlochen Center for the Arts. His debut collection, *Small Talk*, was selected by Derrick Austin for the Hub City Press New Southern Voices Poetry Prize and will be published in 2026.

LAURA CRESTÉ is the author of *In the Good Years* (Four Way Books, 2025) and *You Should Feel Bad*, winner of a 2019 Chapbook Fellowship from the Poetry Society of America. She holds an MFA from New York University and has received fellowships and other support from the Fine Arts Work Center in Provincetown, the Sewanee Writers' Conference, the Tin House Summer Workshop, the Community of Writers, Monson Arts, and the St. Botolph Club Foundation.

BRIAN CZYZYK is a queer poet from Traverse City, Michigan. He holds an MFA from Purdue University and is pursuing a PhD in creative writing at the University of North Texas where he serves as editor-in-chief of *American Literary Review*. A recipient of awards from the Academy of American Poets and AWP, his work is published and forthcoming in *Birmingham Poetry Review*, *The Hopkins Review*, *Cream City Review*, *Waxwing*, *Poetry*, and elsewhere.

KATE DELAY is a poet from Tennessee. A 2025 Pushcart Prize winner, her work can be found or forthcoming in the *The Iowa Review*, *Pleiades*, *swamp pink*, *The Adroit Journal*, *Indiana Review*, and elsewhere. Kate is the winner of the 2023 William Matthews Poetry Prize, selected by Diane Seuss, and she is currently a PhD student in poetry at Florida State University. Find her at katedelaypoet.com.

JONATHAN DIAZ is a poet and assistant professor at Westmont College in Santa Barbara. He is the recipient of the 2024 Pablo Neruda Prize for Poetry from *Nimrod International Journal*. His poetry has also appeared in *AGNI*, *Huizache*, and *Acentos Review*.

COURTNEY DUCHENE is a poet, journalist, and essayist based in Philadelphia, Pennsylvania. She holds an MFA from the Helen Zell Writers' Program at the University of Michigan. Her work has been recognized and supported by the Hopwood Awards, the Vermont Studio Center, Bread Loaf Environmental Writers' Conference, and the Napa Valley Writers' Conference. Her poems, essays and interviews can be found or are forthcoming in *Prairie Schooner*, *The Mississippi Review*, *Frontier*, *RHINO*, *New England Review*, *Philadelphia Stories*, *Glass Mountain*, *Michigan Quarterly Review*, *The Millions*, and *The White Review*, where she was shortlisted for the 2023 Poet's Prize. She was longlisted for the 2023 Rising Poet Prize from *Palette Poetry*.

EMET EZELL is an artist living in Berlin, Germany. Trained in the studio of Robert Sawa, ezell's creative practice spans poetry, papermaking, performance, and print. Recent or forthcoming work can be found in *The American Poetry Review* and *Hand Papermaking Magazine*.

JOSÉ FELIPE OZUNA is a poet living in Minneapolis, Minnesota. He is a 2022 Undocupoets Fellow and a 2023–24 Mentor Series Fellow. His poems are published in *Michigan Quarterly Review*, *The Rumpus*, *Afternoon Visitor*, and the anthology *Here to Stay*. He is working on his first poetry collection.

MCKENDY FILS-AIMÉ is a New England based Haitian-American poet, organizer, and teaching artist. He has received fellowships from Callaloo, Cave Canem, The Watering Hole, and Periplus. Over the span of nearly two decades, Mckendy has represented New England in several regional and national poetry slams, performing on numerous semi-final and final stages. Mckendy's work has been featured or is forthcoming in *The Adroit Journal*, *Muzzle*, *swamp pink*, the Academy of American Poets' Poem-a-Day series, and elsewhere. His debut poetry collection will be published by YesYes Books in 2026.

KATEY FUNDERBURGH (she/her) is a queer Colorado poet. She is a current MFA candidate at George Mason University. Katey serves as a co-coordinator for the Incarcerated Writers Project, and as a Poetry Alive! teaching fellow. Her work appears or is forthcoming in *The Rumpus*, *Inner Forest Service*, and *West Trade Review*.

HARRISON HAMM is a writer and educator from rural Tennessee. His debut chapbook, *If It's Country Music You Want*, won the 2025 Poetry Society of America Chapbook Fellowship and will be published in 2026. Named a finalist for the 2025 Ruth Lily and Dorothy Sargent Rosenberg Poetry Fellowship, his writing appears in *Poetry, The Missouri Review, The Poetry Review, DIAGRAM, Verse Daily*, and more. In 2027, he will earn an MFA in creative writing at New York University as a Goldwater Writing Workshop Fellow.

MICHAEL HURLEY is from Pittsburgh. His work has appeared in or is forthcoming from *The American Poetry Review, Poetry Northwest, Beloit Poetry Journal, Five Points, Copper Nickel, Blackbird, Guernica*, and elsewhere. His chapbook, *Wooden Boys*, is available from Seven Kitchens Press.

L. A. JOHNSON is the author of *Lost Music* (Milkweed Editions, forthcoming 2027) and an associate editor of *Swirl & Vortex: Collected Poems of Larry Levis* (Graywolf Press, 2026). She holds a PhD from University of Southern California, where she was a Mellon Humanities and University of the Future Postdoctoral Fellow. The winner of the 2022 Mississippi Review Poetry Prize, her poems appear in *New England Review, Poetry, Ploughshares*, and elsewhere. She is currently a Hughes Fellow at Southern Methodist University.

TOBI KASSIM's work has been published in *The Volta, Chicago Review, The Rumpus, The Kenyon Review, The Boiler, Obsidian, Four Way Review*, and elsewhere. His work has been supported by an Undocupoets Fellowship, a Stadler Center Undergraduate Fellowship, a Katharine Bakeless Nason Fellowship from the Bread Loaf Writers' Conference, and a Cave Canem Fellowship. He was a finalist for the Furious Flower Poetry Prize and won a Sean T. Lannan Poetry Prize from Yale's English Department. His chapbook, *Dear Sly Stone*, was published by Spiral Editions.

ANYA KIRSHBAUM (she/her) is a bi/queer poet and somatic therapist living in Seattle, Washington. Her work has appeared in *Mississippi Review, Whale Road Review, Crannóg, Solstice Literary Magazine*, and elsewhere. She was a finalist for the New Millennium Writing Awards and the Patricia Dobler Poetry Award, was nominated for a 2024 Forward Prize, and was the recipient of the 2023 Banyan Poetry Prize. She is at work on her first collection.

HANNAH KOSAK is from Long Island, New York. She earned her BA from the Writing Seminars at Johns Hopkins University and is currently an English teaching assistant in France. She recently won the Laureen Rita Schipsi Prize from the Academy of American Poets, judged by Edgar Kunz. Other poems of hers can be found or are forthcoming in *Poet Lore*, *Prism Review*, and *Pinch*.

PETER LABERGE is the author of the chapbooks *Makeshift Cathedral* (YesYes Books) and *Hook* (Sibling Rivalry Press). His poetry has received a Pushcart Prize and has appeared in *AGNI*, *The American Poetry Review*, *The Georgia Review*, *The Kenyon Review*, and *New England Review*, among others. Peter received his BA from the University of Pennsylvania and his MFA from New York University, where he studied as a Writers in the Public Schools Fellow. He is the founder and editor-in-chief of *The Adroit Journal* and lives online at peterlaberge.com.

CAROLINE LAGANAS is earning her PhD in creative writing at Florida State University. She earned an MFA in creative writing from California Institute of the Arts and a BA in journalism from Pepperdine University. She was an International Merit Award winner in the Atlanta Review International Poetry Competition and a finalist for the Mississippi Review Prize. Her poems and translations appear in *Poetry*, *The Los Angeles Review*, *Five Points*, *New Orleans Review*, *Tampa Review*, and many others. She is currently writing and illustrating her first book of poetry while translating an Italian cookbook.

KENT LEATHAM is a poet, translator, public educator, and proud member of the LGBTQIA+ family. Kent's work has appeared in dozens of journals and anthologies in the United States and abroad, including *Best New Poets 2022*. Kent lives in California and curates the Monterey Bay Poetry Consortium monthly reading series.

ALEXANDER LEE is a high school student in South Korea. He is an alumnus of the Iowa Young Writers' Studio and *The Adroit Journal*'s Summer Mentorship Program. His work has been featured in the *Two Hawks Quarterly*, *The Tusculum Review*, and *Polyphony Lit*, as well as the Sarah Mook Poetry Contest.

LINDSAY LI is a Chinese American writer from the Bay Area who loves music, summer, and tanghulu. Her work is published or forthcoming in *Frontier Poetry*, *The Inflectionist Review*, and more. She is currently a poetry reader for *The Adroit Journal*.

JANIRU LIYANAGE is a student and writer. His work has been cited in the Pushcart Prize Anthology, and recently appears in *Poetry*, *AGNI*, *Gulf Coast*, *Black Warrior Review*, *The Slowdown*, and elsewhere. He has produced work for Australian Poetry, the Wheeler Centre, and the Emerging Writers' Festival, among other places.

ELIZABETH LOUDON's work has appeared in, among others, *Blue Mountain Review*, *Amsterdam Review*, *Southword*, *North American Review*, and *Denver Quarterly*. Her debut novel, *A Stranger in Baghdad*, was published in 2023 (AUC Hoopoe). After twenty-five years in Massachusetts, she returned to the United Kingdom. When not writing, she's mostly outside.

ALEJANDRO LUCERO's chapbook, *Sapello Son*, was named the Editors' Selection for the Frost Place Competition (Bull City Press, 2024). His work appears in *Best New Poets 2023*, *Cincinnati Review*, *Ecotone*, *Gulf Coast*, *Missouri Review*, *Southern Review*, and *Verse Daily*. He lives in Baltimore, where he is a Salter Lecturer in the Writing Seminars at Johns Hopkins and a senior editor for *The Hopkins Review*.

CATE LYCURGUS is the author of *Seacliff* (Bull City Press, Fall 2025). Her work has also appeared or is forthcoming in *Best American Poetry*, *The American Poetry Review*, *Ploughshares*, *The Kenyon Review*, and elsewhere. Cate lives in San Jose, California, where she interviews for *32 Poems* and teaches.

BRITTANY MALE is a copywriter living in Richmond, Virginia. She is a graduate of The Ohio State University, where she spent time working at *The Journal*. Her work has appeared in *Glass Mountain*, *Adelaide Literary Magazine*, *SLAB*, and Alternative Field's poetry chapbook *In Isolation: An Anthology*, among other publications.

MELISSA MCKINSTRY hosts quarterly poetry and jazz evenings and curates a community Poet Tree in San Diego. Her poetry appears or is forthcoming in many journals including

Beloit Poetry Journal, The Adroit Journal, and *Narrative Magazine,* and has been selected for the 2025 New Ohio Review Literary Prize and a 2026 Pushcart Prize. An Adroit Djanikian Scholar and the inaugural writer-in-residence at the Millay House Rockland, she currently serves on the Alumni Council for Pacific University's MFA program and the board of the Millay House Rockland.

LENNA MENDOZA is a poet from Texas living in Tucson. Her poems have recently appeared in *Quarterly West, Four Way Review, Salamander, Passages North,* and *The Hudson Review.* She holds an MFA in poetry from the University of Mississippi.

BROOKE MIDDLEBROOK is a writer from western Massachusetts. She received her MFA in nonfiction from Bennington College, and her recent work appears in *The Citron Review, Fugue,* and *Lost Balloon.*

LO NAYLOR is a poet and filmmaker from Salt Lake City. A co-winner of the 2025 Ploughshares Emerging Writer's Contest in Poetry, Lo earned an MFA in poetry from NYU. Recent poems appear or are forthcoming in *Ploughshares, The Missouri Review, The Adroit Journal, Narrative Magazine, Alaska Quarterly Review,* and *Prairie Schooner,* among others. She lives and works in Brooklyn.

JUPITER NESKY (he/she/it) is a mad, queer poet and a sophomore at Kenyon College. From Maryland, she is a co-founder of Young Poets Workshops and a graduate of the Iowa Young Writers Workshop.

SOPHIE PEDERSEN is a Brooklyn-based poet and MFA candidate at NYU's Creative Writing Program. Her work appears in *Lesbians Are Miracles, Black Warrior Review,* and Querencia Press. In 2020, she won Colby College's Elmira Nelson Jones Prize for Outstanding Fiction Writer. She has previously worked as an editor for *Washington Square Review,* and she currently works as a professor at NYU's undergraduate creative writing program.

CHI PHAM is an undergraduate at Rice University. His writing has appeared in *SmokeLong Quarterly* and received commendation for the 2025 Adroit Prize for Poetry. He is from Houston, Texas, and Đồng Nai, Vietnam.

G.H. PLAAG is a poet, a novelist, and an historian's daughter who split her childhood between the woods and the state archives. She received her MFA from Hollins University, where she also taught, is an alumnus of Sundress Academy for the Arts, and has published work with *ANMLY*, *Boulevard*, *Redivider*, *Tahoma Literary Review*, *The Mississippi Review*, and Poets.org, among others. Currently, she resides in New Orleans, where she is developing a novel in conversation with various structures of power along the Gulf Coast.

DORA PRIETO is a Mexican-Canadian poet relocating to Oakland as a 2025–27 Wallace Stegner Fellow at Stanford. Her debut poetry collection is forthcoming with House of Anansi (April 2027) and her book of co-translated poems, *JAWS*, is forthcoming with Cardboard House Press (September 2026). She is a member of El Mashup Collective, and her work has appeared in *Acentos Review*, *Maisonneuve*, *Catapult*, *Capilano Review*, and more.

JUSTIN RIGAMONTI lives in Oregon and teaches English at Portland Community College. His poems have been recently published or are forthcoming in *American Poetry Review*, *Ploughshares*, *Rattle*, *West Trade Review*, and the 2024 anthology *The Poetry of Grief, Gratitude, and Reverence* (Wisdom Books).

RACHEL ROTHENBERG was born in Edison, New Jersey. A recent winner of the Greg Grummer Poetry Prize and the Nancy D. Hargrove Editors' Prize in Poetry, her work is featured or forthcoming in *Shenandoah*, *Salt Hill*, *Poetry Northwest*, *Raleigh Review*, *Jabberwock*, *phoebe*, and elsewhere. She is a PhD candidate at the University of Rhode Island and the senior associate editor at Barrow Street Press.

JACKIE SABBAGH is a writer living in Brooklyn, New York. Her writing has appeared in publications including *AGNI*, *Gulf Coast*, *Ninth Letter*, *Subtropics*, *SmokeLong Quarterly*, and *Poetry*, which awarded her poems the Frederick Bock prize.

JEN SIRAGANIAN is an Armenian-American writer, educator, and former poet laureate of Los Gatos, California. Her poetry has won the New Ohio Review Poetry Prize and appeared in *AGNI*, *Cincinnati Review*, *Cortland Review*, *Electric Literature*, *Poetry Daily*,

Prairie Schooner, and *The Rumpus*. A former managing director of Litquake: San Francisco's Literary Festival, she is a current Lucas Artist Fellow at the Montalvo Arts Center.

MARY SPOONER is a poet from Jackson, Mississippi. Her work has appeared in *The Adroit Journal* and *Memorious*. She received an MFA in poetry from the Helen Zell Writers' Program. Mary lives in Los Angeles and teaches in Writing Programs at UCLA.

D. M. SPRATLEY is a Wallace Stegner Fellow at Stanford University. Her work has also been supported by Cave Canem, the North Carolina Arts Council, Lenoir-Rhyne University, and the William C. Friday Fellowship for Human Relations. Her writing has been featured in *Poetry*, *The Adroit Journal*, *Ecotone*, *Shenandoah*, and elsewhere.

NUR TURKMANI is a writer from Beirut. Her work appears in *Poetry*, *New England Review*, *The Adroit Journal*, and *The Rumpus*. Her debut poetry collection, *October*, is forthcoming with Hajar Press in 2026. She received the Anthony Veasna So Scholarship for her short stories.

BENJAMIN VOIGT grew up on a small farm and the internet. His chapbook *Postpastoral* was selected for the Poetry.onl Chapbook Fellowship and published in 2023. His poems have been published in *AGNI*, *Bennington Review*, *Fence*, *Poetry Northwest*, and *ZYZZYVA*. His criticism has been published in *The Kenyon Review*, *Pleiades*, and on the Poetry Foundation's website. He works at Macalester College and lives in Minneapolis.

GENEVIEVE WATSON is a high school student from Los Angeles, California. Her work has appeared or is forthcoming in *Wildness*, *The Adroit Journal*, and more. She has also been recognized by *The New York Times* and The Adroit Prizes for Poetry and Prose, among others. When she's not writing she enjoys spending time by the beach.

MASON WRAY is a poet from Georgia. His poems appear in journals such as *Ploughshares*, *RHINO*, *New Ohio Review*, and *West Branch*. He is a graduate of the MFA program at Ole Miss and has received support from organizations including Bread Loaf, the Hambidge Center, and The Mount, Edith Wharton's Home. He lives in Atlanta.

Participating Magazines

32 Poems
32poems.com

The Account
theaccountmagazine.com

The Adroit Journal
theadroitjournal.org

AGNI
agnionline.bu.edu

ALOCASIA
alocasia.org

American Literary Review
americanliteraryreview.com

ANMLY
anmly.org

Apple Valley Review
applevalleyreview.org

ARTS & LETTERS
artsandletters.gcsu.edu

Barrelhouse
barrelhousemag.com

Bayou Magazine
bayoumagazine.org

Beestung
beestungmag.com

Bellevue Literary Review
blreview.org

Bellingham Review
bhreview.org

Beloit Poetry Journal
bpj.org

Bennington Review
benningtonreview.org

Birmingham Poetry Review
uab.edu/cas/englishpublications/
    birmingham-poetry-review

Blackbird
blackbird.vcu.edu

Bloodroot
bloodrootlit.org

Booth: A Journal
booth.butler.edu

Cave Wall
cavewallpress.com

Cherry Tree
washcoll.edu/cherrytree

Chestnut Review
chestnutreview.com

Cincinnati Review
cincinnatireview.com

Cutbank
cutbankonline.org

Cutleaf
cutleafjournal.com

Diode
diodepoetry.com

DIALOGIST
dialogist.org

F(r)iction
frictionlit.org

The Fiddlehead
thefiddlehead.ca

Fjords Review
fjordsreview.com

The Florida Review
cah.ucf.edu/floridareview

Foglifter
foglifterjournal.com

The Fourth River
thefourthriver.com

Free State Review
freestatereview.com

Frozen Sea
frozensea.org

Fruitslice
thefruitslice.com

Fugue
fuguejournal.com

The Georgia Review
thegeorgiareview.com

Glass: A Journal of Poetry
glass-poetry.com/journal.html

The Good Life Review
thegoodlifereview.com

Greensboro Review
greensbororeview.org

Hayden's Ferry Review
haydensferryreview.com

Hominum
hominumjournal.org

Honey Literary
honeyliterary.com

The Hopkins Review
hopkinsreview.com

After Happy Hour Review
afterhappyhourreview.com

Image
imagejournal.org

Jet Fuel Review
jetfuelreview.com

The Lascaux Review
lascauxreview.com

Lucky Jefferson
luckyjefferson.com

The MacGuffin
schoolcraft.edu/macguffin

The Margins
aaww.org

Massachusetts Review
massreview.org

The McNeese Review
mcneese.edu/thereview

Michigan Quarterly Review
sites.lsa.umich.edu/mqr

Mississippi Review
www.mississippi-review.com

MORIA Literary Magazine
moriaonline.com

Muzzle Magazine
muzzlemagazine.com

The Nashville Review
as.vanderbilt.edu/nashvillereview

New England Review
nereview.com

New Orleans Review
neworleansreview.org

Nimrod International Journal
artsandsciences.utulsa.edu/nimrod/

Ninth Letter
ninthletter.com

Okay Donkey
okaydonkeymag.com

Passages North
passagesnorth.com

The Penn Review
pennreview.org

Phoebe
phoebejournal.com

Ploughshares
pshares.org

The Pinch
pinchjournal.com

Poet Lore
poetlore.com

$ - Poetry Is Currency
poetrycurrency.com

Posit Journal
positjournal.com

Prism Review
sites.laverne.edu/prism-review

Psaltery & Lyre
psalteryandlyre.org

Radar Poetry
radarpoetry.com

Radon Journal
radonjournal.com

Raleigh Review
RaleighReview.org

Ran Off with the Star Bassoon
ranoffwiththestarbassoon.com

Rat's Ass Review
ratsassreview.net

Rattle
rattle.com

Redivider
redividerjournal.org

Room Magazine
roommagazine.com

Salamander
salamandermag.org

Sapiens
sapiens.org

The Seventh Wave
theseventhwave.co

Sewanee Review
thesewaneereview.com

Shenandoah
shenandoahliterary.org

Shō Poetry Journal
shopoetryjournal.com

SICK
sickmagazine.org

Sine Theta Magazine
sinetheta.net

Sixth Finch
sixthfinch.com

Slab
slablitmag.org

Slippery Elm
slipperyelm.findlay.edu

The Southeast Review
southeastreview.org

The Southern Review
thesouthernreview.org

Split Lip Magazine
splitlipthemag.com

storySouth
storysouth.com

Sugar House Review
SugarHouseReview.com

Sundog Lit
sundoglit.com

SWWIM Every Day
swwim.org

Tahoma Literary Review
tahomaliteraryreview.com

Up the Staircase Quarterly
upthestaircase.org

Variant Literature
variantlit.com

Virginia Quarterly Review
vqronline.org

Washington Square Review
washingtonsquarereview.com

Waxwing Literary Journal
waxwingmag.org

West Trestle Review
westtrestlereview.com

Whale Road Review
whaleroadreview.com

wildness
readwildness.com

wildscape
wildscapelit.com

Witness
witness.blackmountaininstitute.org

The Yale Review
yalereview.org

Participating Programs

Arizona State University MFA in Creative Writing
english.asu.edu/academics/areas-of-study/creative-writing

Binghampton University Creative Writing Program
binghamton.edu/english/creative-writing

Chatham University MFA in Creative Writing
chatham.edu/mfa

City College of New York MFA Program in Creative Writing
ccny.cuny.edu/english/creativewriting

Florida International University MFA in Creative Writing
english.fiu.edu/creative-writing

Hollins University Jackson Center for Creative Writing
hollinsmfa.wordpress.com

Johns Hopkins The Writing Seminars
writingseminars.jhu.edu

Kansas State University MFA in Creative Writing Program
k-state.edu/english/programs/cw

McNeese State University MFA Program
mfa.mcneese.edu

Minnesota State University Mankato Creative Writing Program
english.mnsu.edu/cw

Monmouth University Creative Writing
monmouth.edu/school-of-humanities-social-sciences/ma-english.aspx

New School Writing Program
newschool.edu/writing

New York University Creative Writing Program
as.nyu.edu/cwp

Northwestern University MA/MFA in Creative Writing
sps.northwestern.edu/program-areas/graduate/creative-writing

Pratt Institute MFA in Writing
pratt.edu

San Diego State University MFA in Creative Writing
mfa.sdsu.edu

Sarah Lawrence College MFA in Writing
sarahlawrence.edu/writing-mfa

Southeast Missouri State University Master of Arts in English
semo.edu/english

UMass Amherst MFA for Poets and Writers
umass.edu/englishmfa

UMass Boston MFA Program in Creative Writing
umb.edu/academics/cla/english/grad/mfa

UNC Greensboro Creative Writing Program
mfagreensboro.org

University of Alabama at Birmingham Graduate Theme in Creative Writing
uab.edu/cas/english/graduate-program/creative-writing

University of Connecticut Creative Writing Program
creativewriting.uconn.edu

University of Idaho MFA in Creative Writing
uidaho.edu/class/english/graduate/mfa-creative-writing

University of Maryland MFA Program
english.umd.edu

University of New Orleans Creative Writing Workshop
uno.edu/writing

University of San Francisco MFA in Writing
usfca.edu/mfa

University of Southern Mississippi Center for Writers
usm.edu/writers

University of Texas Michener Center for Writers
michener.utexas.edu

Vermont College of Fine Arts MFA in Writing
vcfa.edu

West Virginia University MFA Program
creativewriting.wvu.edu

The series editor wishes to thank the many poets involved in our first round of reading:

Kate Coleman, Gabriel Costello, Jack Grimes, Lyd Havens, Desiree Hensley, Samuel Nnadi, and Holly Zhou.

Special thanks to Jason Coleman and the University of Virginia Press for their editorial advice and support for this poetry project.